At the Arcade

Understand Place Value

Annie Pomerleau

ROSEN
COMMON CORE MATH
READERS

Rosen Classroom™

New York

Published in 2015 by The Rosen Publishing Group, Inc.
29 East 21st Street, New York, NY 10010

Book Design: Jonathan J. D'Rozario

Photo Credits: Cover PhotoPlus Magzine/Future/Getty Images; p. 5 Leland Bobbe/The Image Bank/Getty Images; p. 7 Stephen Bonk/Shutterstock.com; p. 9 Mark III Photonics/Shutterstock.com; p. 11 Amy Planz/Shutterstock.com; p. 13 RonTech2000/iStock.com; p. 15 Andy Ryan/The Image Bank/Getty Images; p. 17 Dave Higginson/Ikon Images/ Getty Images; p. 19 Philip Lange/Shutterstock.com; p. 21 (main) Susie Adams/Flickr/Getty Images; p. 21 (tickets) shippee/ Shutterstock.com p. 22 indigolotos/Shutterstock.com.

Library of Congress Cataloging-in-Publication Data

Pomerleau, Annie, author.
At the arcade : understand place value / Annie Pomerleau.
pages cm. — (Math masters. Number and operations in base ten)
Includes index.
ISBN 978-1-4777-4660-8 (pbk.)
ISBN 978-1-4777-4661-5 (6-pack)
ISBN 978-1-4777-6430-5 (library binding)
1. Place value (Mathematics)—Juvenile literature. 2. Addition—Juvenile literature. 3. Arcades—Juvenile literature.
I. Title.
QA141.15.P66 2015
513.2'1—dc23

2013042787

Manufactured in the United States of America

CPSIA Compliance Information: Batch #WS15RC: For further information contact Rosen Publishing, New York, New York at 1-800-237-9932.

Contents

Let's Celebrate!

Audrey enjoys playing games at her local **arcade**. She loves to play the older games, such as basketball and pinball. She also likes the newer video games. But Audrey's mom says she can only go if she keeps her grades up. Audrey does very well on her math test, so her mom says she can go to the arcade to **celebrate**.

Audrey thinks the arcade is a great place to practice math. She wants to practice skip-counting.

Shooting Hoops

In math class, Audrey learned that skip-counting is when you count by numbers other than 1. This helps her count big numbers faster. Audrey already knows how to count by 2s. Today, she wants to practice skip-counting by bigger numbers. The first game she plays is basketball. She earns 5 points for each basket.

Audrey earns 30 points. She skip-counts to 30 by 5s. When Audrey skip-counts by 5s, the ones place switches from 0 to 5 and then back to 0.

5, 10, 15, 20, 25, 30

It takes good **aim** to make a basket. Basketball is good practice for skip-counting by 5s. Audrey decides to play again. This time, she makes 8 baskets. She skip-counts her points: 5, 10, 15, 20, 25, 30, 35, 40. That's a lot of points! She plays 1 more time, and she makes 11 baskets. How many points does she earn?

Audrey counts up to 55 points by 5s.

5, 10, 15, 20, 25, 30, 35, 40, 45, 50, 55

Skip-Counting Skee Ball

Audrey likes skip-counting by 10s because it's very easy. It's like counting by 1, except the tens place changes and the ones place stays the same. A good game to practice counting by 10s is skee ball. In skee ball, a player rolls a ball up a ramp. The player needs to get the ball into one of the holes to score points.

Different holes count for different points. Audrey earns 40 points by shooting 4 balls into 10-point holes.

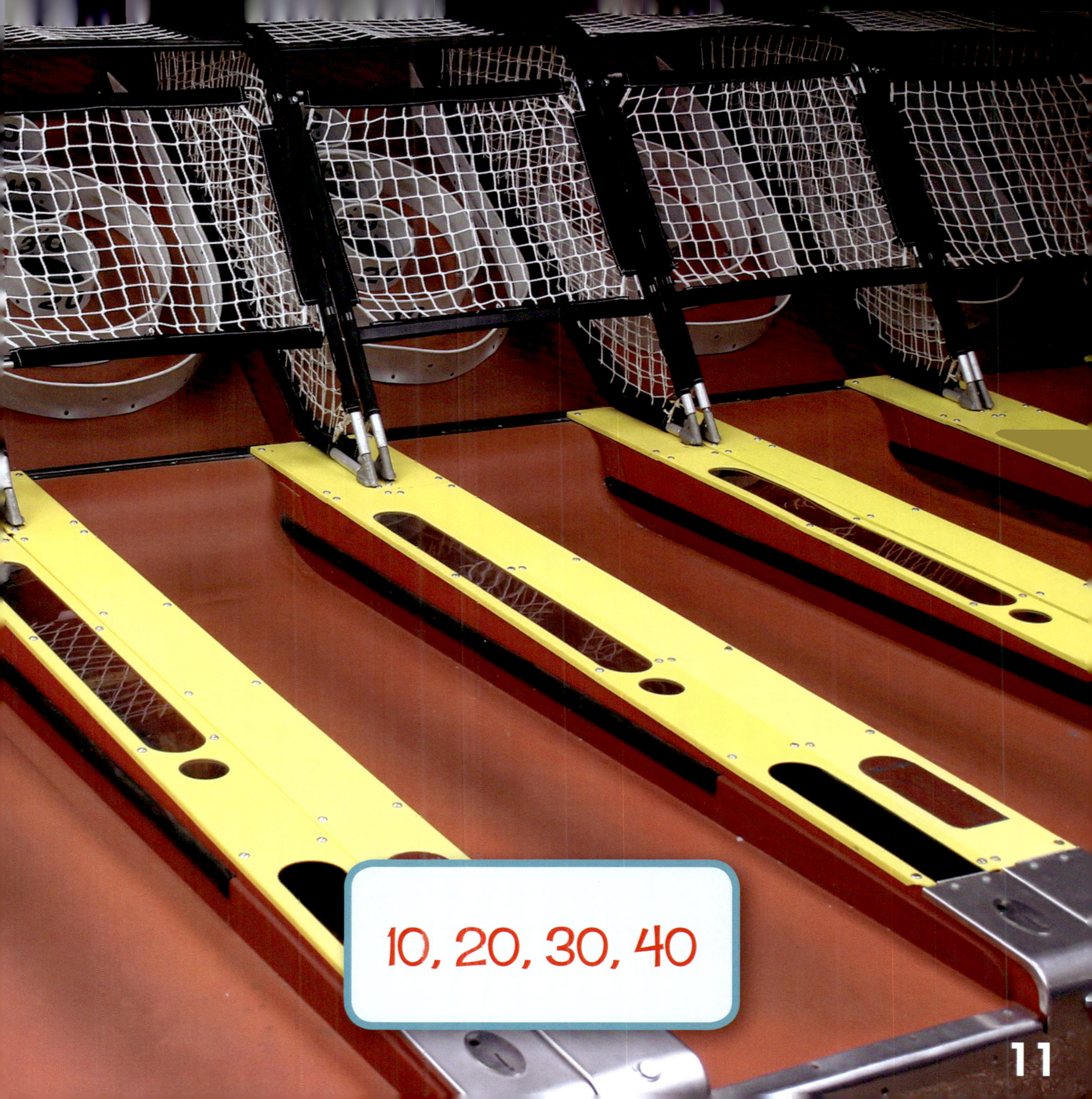

10, 20, 30, 40

Audrey wants to see how many more times she can roll the ball into the 10-point hole. On her next game, she rolls the ball into the 10-point hole 6 times. To count her points, Audrey skip-counts by 10s. She's earned 60 points! Audrey adds the 40 points from her first game to the 60 points from her second game for a total of 100 points.

How many times does 10 go into 100? You can skip-count to find out.

10, 20, 30, 40, 50, 60, 70, 80, 90, 100

Audrey's older brother Josh is very good at skee ball. Audrey wants to see if he can roll all 100s today, so she can practice skip-counting by 100. Josh has very good aim, so he rolls all 6 balls into the 100-point hole. They count his score together: 100, 200, 300, 400, 500, 600. He made 600 points altogether.

Josh wins a lot of tickets playing skee ball. He can use the tickets to pick out a big prize!

100, 200, 300, 400, 500, 600

Other Games

Audrey's favorite game at the arcade is pinball. She's very good at it, so she can earn a lot of points. In pinball, a player shoots a tiny ball into a machine with many **targets**. Every time the ball hits a target, the player earns points. By the end of her first game, Audrey earns 300 points.

Audrey counts to 300 by 100s!

100, 200, 300

Basketball, skee ball, and pinball are **classic** arcade games. But this arcade has newer games too, including many different video games. Audrey earns 400 points on 1 of the video games, and Josh wins 300. Together, they earn 700 points. Audrey wants to skip-count by 100s. How many 100s are there in the number 700? How do you know?

Audrey counts 7 groups of 100 in the number 700.

TRUCKS
RACING
App Store

Winning a Prize

The best part of going to the arcade is getting a prize. First, Audrey needs to count all her tickets. Audrey could count the tickets by 5s or 10s, but it would take a long time. She thinks it would be best to split the tickets into groups of 100. She has 9 groups of 100. Can you skip-count by 100s to 900?

Audrey has 40 tickets left over. Can you skip-count to 40 by 10s? How about by 5s?

TICKET
338950
338949

Audrey has many prizes to choose from. She can get a bouncy ball for 800 tickets. Or she can get a sticker book for 700 tickets. She can get sunglasses for 1,000 tickets. Audrey wants the sunglasses, but she doesn't have enough tickets. Josh tells Audrey he'll give her the extra tickets she needs. Audrey is so excited to take home a good prize!

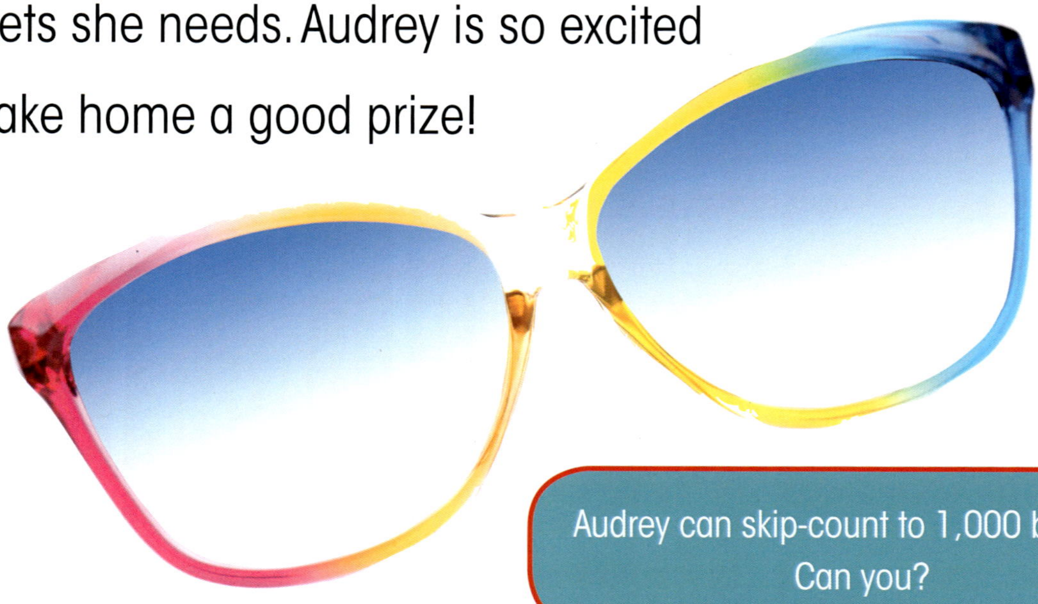

Audrey can skip-count to 1,000 by 100s. Can you?

Glossary

aim (AYM) The ability to hit a target.

arcade (ahr-KAYD) A place with games that you pay to play.

celebrate (SEH-luh-brayt) To honor something or make it special by doing things that people enjoy.

classic (KLA-sihk) Popular over a long period of time.

target (TAHR-guht) Something you want to hit.

Index

Due to the changing nature of Internet links, The Rosen Publishing Group, Inc., has developed an online list of websites related to the subject of this book. This site is updated regularly. Please use this link to access the list: **www.powerkidslinks.com/nobt/arca**

DANS MA COMMUNAUTÉ

LES PROFESSIONNELS DE MA VILLE

COLLECTION CRABTREE « LES JEUNES PLANTES »

Taylor Farley

CRABTREE
PUBLISHING COMPANY
WWW.CRABTREEBOOKS.COM

pompier / pompière

E 4

médicin / médecine

enseignant / enseignante

policier / policière

2400
SEATTLE POLICE

bibliothécaire

FICTION

vétérinaire

facteur / factrice

UNITED STATES
POSTAL SERVICE

électricien / électricienne

maire / mairesse

infirmier / infirmière

Glossaire

bibliothécaire (bi-bli-o-té-kèr) : Un bibliothécaire est une personne qui est en charge d'une bibliothèque. Un bibliothécaire peut s'occuper des livres d'une bibliothèque et aider les gens à trouver des informations.

électricien (é-lek-tri-sien) : Un électricien est une personne qui est formée pour assembler et réparer l'équipement électrique. Il peut travailler sur des fils électriques et des machines qui utilisent l'électricité.

enseignant (en-sè-nyan) : Un enseignant est une personne dont le travail consiste à aider les écoliers à apprendre de nouvelles choses.

facteur (fak-teur) : Un facteur est une personne dont le travail est de distribuer et de ramasser le courrier.

infirmier (in-fir-mié) : Un infirmier est formé pour prendre soin des gens qui sont malades ou blessés.

maire (mèr) : Un maire est une personne qui est en charge d'une ville. Le maire est habituellement élu. Cela veut dire que des gens votent pour lui.

médecin (méd-sèn) : Un médecin est une personne qui est formée pour traiter ceux qui sont malades ou blessés. Les médecins prescrivent des médicaments.

policier (po-li-sié) : Un policier est une personne dont le travail consiste à s'assurer que les gens sont en sécurité et suivent les lois. Les lois sont des règlements faits par le gouvernement.

pompier (pon-pié) : Un pompier est formé pour éteindre ou arrêter les incendies. Le pompier sauve également les personnes et les animaux des incendies.

vétérinaire (vé-té-ri-nèr) : Le vétérinaire est aussi appelé : le vet. Un vétérinaire est une personne qui est formée pour soigner les animaux qui sont malades ou blessés.

Index

Soutien de l'école à la maison pour les gardien(ne)s et les enseignant(e)s.

Ce livre aide les enfants à se développer grâce à la pratique de la lecture. Voici quelques exemples de questions pour aider le(a) lecteur(-trice) à développer ses capacités de compréhension. Des suggestions de réponses sont indiquées.

Avant la lecture

- Quel est le sujet de ce livre? Je pense que ce livre parle des personnes qui en aident d'autres. Sur la couverture, je vois un policier, un pompier, une infirmière, un facteur et une vétérinaire.
- Qu'est-ce que je veux savoir sur ce sujet? Je veux en savoir plus sur les différents métiers que les gens font pour aider les autres.

Durant la lecture

- Je me demande pourquoi... Je me demande pourquoi le pompier transporte une hache.
- Qu'est-ce que j'ai appris jusqu'à présent? J'ai appris que les médecins, les enseignants, les bibliothécaires, les électriciens et les maires aident les gens.

Après la lecture

- Nomme quelques détails que tu as retenus. J'ai appris que les gens dépendent d'autres personnes dans leur ville.
- Écris les mots peu familiers et pose des questions pour mieux comprendre leur signification. Je vois le mot ***bibliothécaire*** à la page 10 et le mot ***électricien*** à la page 18. Les autres mots de vocabulaire se trouvent aux pages 22 et 23.

Crabtree Publishing Company
www.crabtreebooks.com 1–800–387–7650

Version imprimée du livre produite conjointement avec Blue Door Education en 2021.

Crédits photos : Illustration de personnes © Maciej Es; illustration de personnes © tynyuk; couverture et p. 3 © Shutterstock.com / Digital Storm; couverture et p. 5 © Shutterstock.com/ Oksana Kuzmina; p. 7 © Shutterstock.com /Rawpixel.com; couverture et p. 9 ©Shutterstock.com/Harry Hu; p. 11 ©Shutterstock.com/ChameleonsEye; p 13 ©Shutterstock.com/Pressmaster; p. 15 © Shutterstock.com / Lucky Business; p. 17 ©Shutterstock.com/Peter Titmuss; p. 19 shutterstock.com/ Biserka Stojanovic; p. 23 Shutterstock.com/ monkeybusinessimages; p. 21 shutterstock.com/ shironosov

Imprimé au Canada/042021/CPC

Auteur : Taylor Farley
Coordinatrice à la production et technicienne au prepress : Amy Salter
Coordinatrice à l'impression : Katherine Berti
Traduction : Claire Savard

Publié au Canada par Crabtree Publishing
616 Welland Ave.
St. Catharines, ON
L2M 5V6

Publié aux États-Unis par Crabtree Publishing
347 Fifth Ave
Suite 1402-145
New York, NY 10016

Catalogage avant publication de Bibliothèque et Archives Canada

Disponible à Bibliothèque et Archives Canada